The Way of the Househusband

KOUSUKE OONO

9

CONTENTS

CHAPTER 73
DING DONG
DING DONG
DING DONG
YAWN... WHO THE HELL'S LAYIN' ON MY DOOR-BELL?
ALL RIGHT AL-READY!
GCHAK
WHAD-DAYA WANT?!
SURPRISE INSPEC-TION.
WHOA!

YOU SCARED ME, BOSS.
I WAS PASSIN' THROUGH THE AREA. FIGURED I'D DROP IN, SEE WHETHER YOU'RE KEEPIN' UP ON YER CHORES...
RANK.
HUH?! IS IT?
SHIBAINU
SHIBAINU
OH, THAT'S JUST THE MOISTURE THAT ACCUMULATES BY THE FRONT DOOR. IT'S COOL.
C'MON IN AND I'LL BUST OUT SOME TEA.

LOOKS LIKE YOU'VE KEPT THE PLACE PRETTY CLEAN...
STANKY.
Y-YEAH? YOU THINK?
JUST GONNA SETTLE DOWN HERE...
RIPE!
C'MON, DUDE, IT AIN'T *THAT* BAD.
GET YER SNIFFER CHECKED, KID. REEKS LIKE DEATH...
...IN HERE!
D-DOES NOT!

WET SHOES.
THE SINK.
THE TRASH.
HANGING CLOTHES TO DRY INSIDE.
the machine
ALL OF THESE FACTIONS—THE DIFFERENT HOUSEHOLD ODORS—ARE INTER-LOCKED...
ODOR
...IN A TRICKY TURF WAR!

I'VE GOT JUST THE THING...
KLAK
...TO TURN THIS BATTLE AROUND!
HERBS.
WHERE'D YOU SCORE SO MUCH BUD?!
THE FIVE-AND-DIME.

COMBINE BAKING SODA AND ESSENTIAL OILS...
ECO-FRIENDLY
...FOR A TOP-QUALITY PRODUCT-DEODORIZER!
H-HERE WE GO! IT'S THE BOSS'S BEST SCHTICK!
THE "MIX WHITE POWDER WITH JUNK" THING!
TUG
AS A BONUS, IF YOU TIE A RIBBON AROUND THE JAR, IT DOUBLES AS A CUTE DECORATION.
SWEET!

FWSH
NEXT.
TUG
CHOOSE THE STRAIN YA WANT TO GIVE YA THAT BUZZ...
...AND BUNDLE 'EM TOGETHER INTO HERB WREATHS!

ALL DONE!
IS IT CUTE?
UH... SURE!
YOURS IS TOO.
HEY, I GOT NUTHIN' ON YOU, BOSS! *HEH HEH!*

FORTIFY YOUR BED-ROOM...
...WITH A LAVENDER WREATH!
HEY, THAT SMELLS KINDA NICE.
LAVENDER LOOSENS UP YOUR SYMPA-THETIC NERVOUS SYSTEM...
...HELPING YOU TO RELAX AND IMPROVE YOUR SLEEP QUALITY.

FOR THE RESTROOM, BLUE ICE CYPRESS!
RIGHT, THIS ONE'S GOT THAT... UH, YOU KNOW...
...THAT NICE SMELL.
THE CYPRESS SCENT WILL HAVE YA FEELIN' LIKE YOU'RE OUT IN THE WOODS TAKIN' IN THE FRESH AIR, ALL WHILE SITTIN' ON THE CAN!
SHIBAINU

PEPPERMINT IS PERFECT FOR THE KITCHEN.
OH! YEAH, YEAH, I KNOW THIS ONE!
IT SMELLS GOOD.
MINT'S RE-FRESHING AROMA...
...MAKES YOU FEEL SO RENEWED...
...IT CAN RESET YOUR ENTIRE MOOD!

AH.
SKITR
ROACH ALERT.
WHAT?!
HA HA HA... DON'T PANIC!
PEPPERMINT'S ALSO AN INSECT REPELLENT.
IT'S SO POTENT IT'LL LEAVE EVEN THE BLACK BULLET QUAKIN' IN HIS BOOTS!

GOT 'IM.
THE HELL YOU DOIN', SLIM?!
CHILL. THIS PLACE GETS ROACHES ALL THE TIME.
SWF
EASY ...
... MASA.
GRP
DON'T MOVE A MUS-CLE!
HUH?

AH!
I MISSED.
UH...
YEAH.
GOOD OL' VENTILATION...
...IS VITAL TOO.

The Way of the Househusband

CHAPTER 74

LATELY I'VE BEEN HOOKED ON NEEDLE FELTING.
OH, THAT'S CUTE!
NEEDLE FELT-ING?
YOU HOLD A NEEDLE LIKE THIS AND POKE A BUNCH OF TIMES ...
...TO ADD COLOR AND SHAPE.
AH, LIKE TATTOO-ING.
NO.

DREAMZ CRAFT STORE
FELT
"MAKE YOUR VERY OWN, ONE-OF-A-KIND CAT..."
MAKE YOUR VERY OWN, ONE-OF-A-KIND CAT WITH NEEDLE FELTING!
INCLUDES INSTRUCTIONS WITH EASY-TO-FOLLOW COLOR PHOTOS.
CALICO CAT
I COULD GIVE IT TO MIKU. WOULD SHE LIKE THAT?

WHERE THE HELL...
...IS IT?
!
THEY'VE GOT TO HAVE A CAT KIT SOME-WHERE.
SWF
LOOKING FOR THIS, MS. TORII?
MAKE YOUR VERY OWN ONE-OF-A-KIND CAT WITH NEEDLE FELTING!
INCLUDES INSTRUCTIONS WITH EASY-TO-FOLLOW COLOR PHOTOS
CALICO CAT

I-I DON'T KNOW WHAT YOU'RE TALKING ABOUT!
WHAT MAKES YOU THINK I'D BE INTERESTED IN THAT CRAP?
THERE ARE ONLY TWO LEFT.
SWIPE
FINE!
I'LL TAKE THE KID UNDER MY WING!
MAKE YOUR VERY OWN ONE-OF-A-KIND CAT WITH NEEDLE FELTING!

HOLD IT!
AND YOU CALL YOURSELF A MAN?
HOW 'BOUT YOU FINISH WHAT YOU STARTED ...
...AND TEACH ME HOW TO MAKE THIS THING?!

GLUE

HOW'S YOURS COMIN' ALON—
DON'T UNDERES-TIMATE ME.
A LITTLE NEEDLE-WORK'S NEVER STOPPED ME BE-FORE.
HUH?
MS. TORII, MIND IF I SEE THAT FOR A MINUTE?
SMAK
DON'T YOU DARE LAY HANDS ON ONE OF MINE!

RAT TAT TAT
S...
TAT
SO FAST!
HE'S SWITCHING NEEDLES ACCORDING TO EACH ONE'S SPECIFIC PURPOSE!
TAT
TA
TAT
TA
TAT
TAT
TA
TAT
THE SHEER NUMBER OF STABS IS ON ANOTHER LEVEL!
TAT
TAT

TATSU, THE IMMORTAL DRAGON...
HIS HUNTER'S INSTINCTS...
...ARE AS SHARP AS EVER!

SHIBAINU
MS. TORII.
CONSIDER YOURSELF AVENGED.
SNRRRF!
SNRRRF!
MS. TORII ?!

IT TOOK A WHILE...
...BUT YOU'VE SHAPED UP WELL.
SNFF ...
HFF...
WELCOME TO THE FAMILY...
...HANAKO.

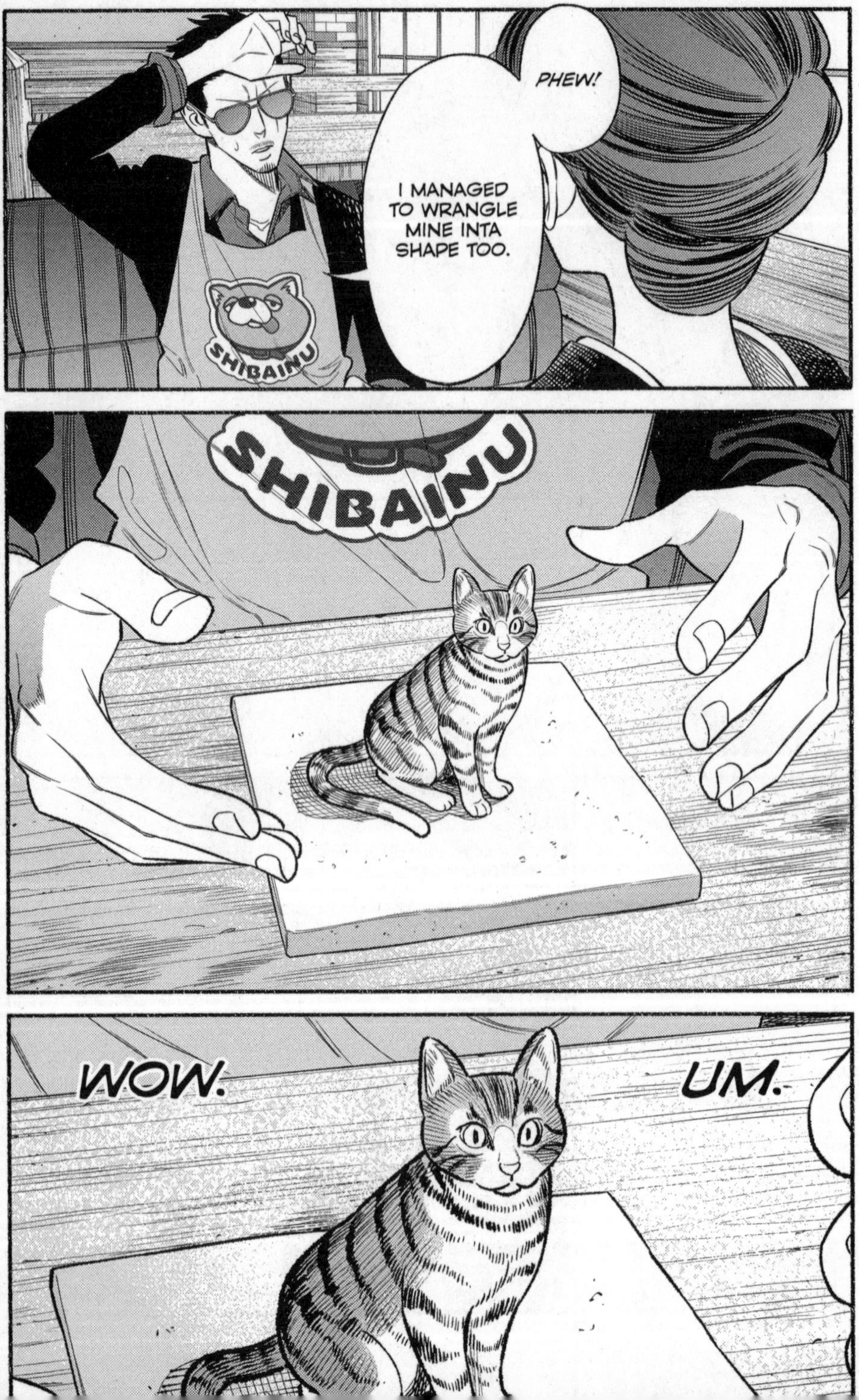
PHEW!
I MANAGED TO WRANGLE MINE INTA SHAPE TOO.
SHIBAINU
SHIBAINU
UM.
WOW.

The Way of the Househusband

CHAPTER 75

AS THE NATION IS COVERED BY A HIGH-PRESSURE SYSTEM...
MAPO BOWL MEAL
FRIED CHICKEN PLATE
780
ASSORTED FRIED FOODS PLATE
830
25TH TODAY'S HIGH TEMPS
KYOTO
39℃
FUKUSHIMA
38℃
HITA
38℃
KOFU
38℃
NATIONWIDE HEAT WAVE
KEEP HYDRATED
...THE HEAT WAVE CONTINUES, WITH TEMPERATURES UPWARDS OF 35°C...
WAKA

IT'S HOT...
I GOTTA GET THIS THING OFFA ME.
DUMBASS!
WE PATROL OUR TURF IN OUR SUITS TO BE SEEN!
HOW'S TAKIN' 'EM OFF GONNA HELP?!
HUH?!
HISS!
BOSS, THAT'S A CAT!

MIND IF WE COOL OFF INSIDE THIS CAFE FOR A BIT, BOSS?
HMPH... F-FINE, WHATEVER.
FIORE
FIORE
I'M SO SORRY. WE'RE FULL AT THE MOMENT.
WHAM
BOSS!

IT'S A VEND-ING MA-CHINE!
WATER!
WE'RE SAVED!
100 YEN
COLD 100 YEN COLD 100 YEN 100
SOLD OUT
SOLD OUT
SOLD OUT
MELON
REFRESHING GRAPE
0 YEN COLD 100 YEN COLD
SOLD OUT
SOLD OUT
WAM
BOSS!

HEY, *PALS.*
LOSE YER COOL LIKE THAT AND YER GONNA DRAW HEAT...
*HEAT*STROKE FROM THIS BLAZIN' SUN, I MEAN.
T...
TATSU, THE IMMORTAL DRAGON?!
YOU THINK *YAKUZA* GET HEAT-STROKE?!
BUZZ OFF!

I'LL SLIP YOU FELLAS SOME GOOD PRODUCT.
LIGHTLY PICKLED CUCUMBERS.
COLD
PICKLE
PERFECT
DAMNY TASTY FOODS
KEEP REFRIGERATED
THE HELL IS THIS?
THOSE BABIES CONTAIN A HIT...
...OF WATER CONTENT AND SALT. IT'LL HELP YA HYDRATE!
KRNCH
KRNCH
KRNCH
KRNCH
KRNCH
YUM!

YOU BOYS GOTTA TAKE BETTER CARE OF YERSELVES, IF YA KNOW WHAT I MEAN.
WHAT YOU NEED IS ONE HIT OF *THIS* EVERY MORNING.
KRNCH
KRNCH
KRNCH
GETS THE BRAIN BUZZED IN NO TIME.
IT'S MISO SOUP.
SOUP?! IN THIS HEAT WAVE ?!

IT'S GOT MINERALS. IT'S GOT WATER CONTENT.
HOT!
THE PUMPKIN CHUNKS ARE FULL OF VITAMINS.
THIS'LL HELP WIPE AWAY FATIGUE!
FUU!
SLURP!
IT'LL KEEP YER INSIDES FROM GETTIN' ICED TOO.
IT'S HOT AS HELL.

I JUST SCORED SOME PRODUCT AT A DISCOUNT.
PROD-UCTS FOR BEATIN' THE HEAT.
LONG-LASTING COLD
COOL!!
COOLING TOWEL
TRIPLE EFFECTIVE
EVAPORATES MOISTURE
ABSORBS HEAT
LONG-LASTING
HAND FAN
MEN

SHIBAINU
WE WEAR OUR SUITS INTO BATTLE.
THEY DON'T COME OFF...
...TILL WE'RE DEAD!

I'M GONNA NEED YOU TO COME WITH ME TO FINISH THE JOB!
JOB ?!
PEACEMART
BAM
SHIBAINU

GROCERY STORES SLINGIN' FRESH FOODS...
...ALWAYS KEEP THE AIR CONDITIONING ON!
野菜 VEGETABLE 果物 FRESH FRUITS
SHIBAINU
PLUS, YOU CAN SHOP FOR DINNER.
IT'S KILLIN' TWO BIRDS WITH ONE STONE.
CABBAGE
ASPARAGUS
OKRA
EGG-PLANT'S IN SEA-SON. IT'S A STEAL!
LET'S BUY SOME, BOSS!
LOOKS LIKE WE'RE HAVIN' EGGPLANT STEW FOR DINNER TONIGHT, BOYS!

CHILLIN'

The Way of the Househusband

CHAPTER 76

THIS IS A TRUE STORY...
...FROM WHEN I WAS STILL A FRESH-FACED EMPLOYEE IN MY FIRST YEAR AT MY COMPANY...

I WAS AT THE OFFICE AFTER EVERYONE HAD LEFT, PUTTING TOGETHER A PRESENTATION ...
...FOR THE NEXT DAY.
WHEN SUD-DENLY...
...MY COMPUT-ER WAS ACTING STRANGE.
I SENSED SOMETHING TERRIBLE. BUT BEFORE I COULD REACT...
...I WAS FROZEN IN PLACE.
PARA-LYZED.

I BROKE OUT...
...IN A COLD SWEAT.
"SOME-BODY..."
"... HELP!"
"HEEELP!" I YELLED, TO NO AVAIL.
I DON'T KNOW HOW MUCH TIME PASSED...
...WHILE MY COMPUTER WAS *COMPLETELY FROZEN*.

OUTSIDE, THE SKY BEGAN TO LIGHTEN...
NAH.
MISS, HOLD UP!
NOT *THAT* KINDA SCARY STORY!
HUH? BUT THIS *IS* SCARY.
WE DID SAY WE WERE GONNA SWAP *GHOST* STORIES, RIGHT?
I'MMA BE STRAIGHT WITH YOU GUYS, THIS NEXT STORY...
...IS PROLLY SAFER LEFT UNTOLD...

I HEARD THIS STORY BACK HOME...
...SEVERAL YEARS AGO FROM THIS OLDER GUY I KNEW.
THERE WAS THIS PLACE THAT WAS INFAMOUS IN THE AREA FOR BEING HAUNTED.
THIS GUY AND SOME OF HIS PALS HAD DECIDED TO CHECK IT OUT. YOLO AND ALL THAT.
SO OFF THEY WENT TO...
WHAT'S IT CALLED?
YOU KNOW, LIKE A BUILDING THAT AIN'T USED ANYMORE... STARTS WITH AN "A"?
ABANDONED. THAT'S IT. AN ABANDONED BUILDING.

ANYWAY, SO THEY HEAD IN, AND AS THEY'RE WALKIN' DOWN THIS NARROW HALL-WAY...
...EVEN THOUGH IT'S THE DEAD OF SUMMER ...
...ONE OF 'EM STARTS SHAKIN' ...
...AND GOIN' ON ABOUT HOW HE'S FREEZIN' HIS ASS OFF.
THE OTHERS ARE LIKE, THAT'S RIDIC. WHAT'S HIS DEAL?
SO THEY FLASH HIM WITH THE, UH... YOU KNOW... ONE OF THOSE THINGS.
YOU PRESS A BUTTON AND BING, THE LIGHT GOES ON?
THEY FLASH MR. FREEZE WITH THAT THING.

THAT'S WHEN THEY SEE IT BEHIND HIM...
... WEARIN' A, YOU KNOW ...
ONE A THOSE WHATCHAMA-CALLITS...LIKE, YOU THROW IT ON AND YOU'RE GOOD, THAT'S ALL YOU NEED?
THIS WOMAN WITH LONG HAIR WEARING ONE A THOSE IS STOOD BEHIND HIM.
THE DUDES ARE LIKE, "WHAT THE HELL? THAT AIN'T RIGHT."
CUZ THIS CHICK, SHE'S AS TALL AS A... WHAT WAS IT AGAIN...
I DUNNO, BUT SHE COULD GIVE AN NBA PLAYER A RUN FOR HIS MONEY.

THE NEXT MOMENT, *BAM!*
SHE'S GOT HER HANDS, LIKE... SHE'S RUSHIN' 'EM ON ALL FOURS LIKE AN ANIMAL...
...AND THEY'RE LIKE, "HOLY CRAP!"
NEXT THING THEY KNOW, *WHAM!* EVERYTHING GOES DARK AND SILENT...
AND WHEN THEY COME TO, IT'S MORNING.
THEY WAKE UP IN ONE OF THOSE ...
WHADDAYA CALL 'EM? ONE OF THOSE LOTS WITH A BUNCHA PARKED CARS. THE END.
I'M GONNA BE STRAIGHT WITH YOU. THAT WAS KINDA CONFUSING.

I COULDN'T FOLLOW THE STORY.
WHAT EXACTLY HAPPENED IN THE SECOND HALF?
THAT'S WHEN, LIKE, THINGS GOT REAL.
GUESS I'M UP LAST.
THIS IS A TRUE STORY OF MY ENCOUNTER WITH A CURSE OF SORTS...
IT ALL WENT DOWN ONE RAINY DAY...
...IN THE VERY RECENT PAST...

I WAS HAVIN' A SNOOZE...
...WHEN I HEARD SOME CHEERFUL MUSIC COMIN' FROM THE TV.
HOKKAIDO SNOW CRAB.
HOKKAIDO SNOW CRAB 3 FOR ¥10,000
ACT NOW AND GET THREE FOR THE LOW PRICE OF 10,000 YEN!
THAT'S WHEN A CHILL RAN DOWN MY SPINE, LIKE THERE WAS A GUN POINTING ...
...AT THE BACK OF MY HEAD.
CUZ OF WHAT A *STEAL* THAT PRICE WAS!

I WAS BESET BY THE SHAKES—*IMPULSE-BUY* SHAKES.
JUST WHEN I THOUGHT THEY'D PASSED...
AND THAT'S NOT ALL!
HOKKAIDO SNOW CRAB: 3 FOR ¥10,000
SPECIAL DEAL! ONE MORE FOR THE SAME PRICE!!!
FOR A LIMITED TIME, WE'LL THROW IN A *FOURTH* ...
...FOR THE SAME PRICE!
IT'S TERRIFYING HOW DEALERS WILL HOOK YA.
I WAS BUYIN' THAT PRODUCT BEFORE I KNEW IT.

A FEW DAYS LATER, THE GOODS ARRIVED.
I WENT TO STASH 'EM AWAY IN THE FREEZER...
...HOLDIN' IN MY EXCITEMENT FOR WHEN I'D GET TO TEAR INTO 'EM.
THAT'S WHEN I NOTICED SOMETHIN' STRANGE.
DEEP IN THE FREEZER WAS A FROST-COVERED ZIPLOCK BAG...

THAT'S RIGHT.
Snow Crab
I'D FORGOTTEN THAT...I'D ORDERED THE SAME EXACT THING ONE YEAR EARLIER.
I TREMBLED WITH FEAR.
THIS WAS THE CURSE...
...OF THE BURIED-ALIVE CRABS!

THAT'S NO CURSE.
THAT'S PLAIN OL' FORGETFULNESS.
FORGIVE ME, CRABS...
AS FOR THE CRAB I GOT THIS YEAR...
...I MADE US A CRAB HOT POT!
YAY!
SHIBAINU

The Way of the Househusband

KATAGI PARK
THAT'S THE TARGET?
CHAPTER 77
THAT'S RIGHT. HER NAME'S SUZU. SHE'S FIVE YEARS OLD.
SHE'S MY DARLING DAUGHTER.

YOU ALSO NEED TO SEE THIS...
daft punk
SHIBAINU
SUZU *HATES* VEGETA-BLES...
...AND I'M A BAD COOK.
I'M DES-PERATE...
...TO GET THAT GIRL TO EAT HER VEGGIES.
CAN I TAKE THAT TO MEAN I HAVE FREE REIGN TO DO WHATEVER IT TAKES TO GET THE JOB DONE?

HEYA, SUZU! WHATCHA PLAYIN' THERE?
I'M COOKING!
HERE, EAT UP!
HOT DAMN, IS THAT A HAM-BURGER STEAK?
CHEW, CHEW. MM!
THAT'S SOME TOP-QUALITY PRODUCT.
IT'S GOT ME BLITZED OUTTA MY MIND!

ALL IT'S MISSIN' IS...
...SOME *CARROTS* OR SOMETHIN' TO ADD SOME COLOR.
WHAT...
...DID YOU JUST SAY?
ER...
A LITTLE COLOR WOULD—
BEFORE THAT.

C... CARROTS?
DON'T EVER SPEAK THAT NAME IN FRONT OF ME AGAIN.
Y-YES, BOSS!

I WON'T LIE TO YA—THE TARGET'S GOOD.
THAT AIN'T THE AURA OF AN AMATEUR.
I KNOW.
SHE'LL BREAK YOUR HEART WITHOUT EVEN BLINKING AN EYE.
WE CAN'T GET COLD FEET.
THIS JOB IS DO-OR-DIE.
SHIBAINU

OH, LI'L LADY! IT'S TIME FOR LUNCH!
I PRESENT TO YOU MY PATENTED KIDDIE MEAL.
WOW! IT LOOKS SO YUMMY!
I LOVE HAM-BURGER STEAK!
YOU DIDN'T SLIP ANYTHING *FISHY* IN HERE, DID YOU?

W...
WOULDN'T DREAM OF IT!
THAT PATTY IS NOTHIN' LESS THAN 100 PERCENT...
...UNCUT BEEF!
THEN WHAT DO YOU CALL THESE ONIONS? HMMM?
SHE CAUGHT ON...
...EVEN AFTER WE CHOPPED IT UP THAT SMALL?!

H... HOW 'BOUT ...
...SOME CURRY? I HEARD YA LOVE CURRY TOO!
THIS CURRY IS...
I SMELL IT.
YOU MAY HAVE TURNED IT INTO A PASTE AND BOILED IT, BUT ...
... THERE'S CARROT IN HERE, ISN'T THERE?
THIS KID'S GOT THE NOSE OF A DRUG-DETECTION DOG!

GREEN PEPPER.
MUSTARD SPINACH.
AH...
NO...
DID YOU THINK YOU'D GET AWAY WITH IT?
WITH A BUST RATE...
...OF 100 PERCENT!

ANY...
...LAST WORDS?
WHY, YOU!

MR. CARROT WAS GROWN WITH TLC BY A FARMER.
HE GREW UP FAST.
BUT NO MATTER WHAT HE DID...
...THE LITTLE KIDDIES ALL HAD BEEF WITH HIM.
MR. CARROT NEEDED TO COOK UP A SCHEME...
...TO GET THE KIDS TO LIKE HIM.

SO HE CAME TO ME ASKIN' FOR A FAVOR.
"KIDS LOVE CURRY."
"PLEASE PUT ME IN CURRY."
"THAT WAY, THEY'LL EAT ME."
AFTER HE'D MADE HIS CASE...
...HE GAVE A SMALL, SAD SMILE.

MR. CARROT ...
I GUESS I CAN EAT A LITTLE—
THEN, MR. CARROT...
...GOT EVISCERATED IN THE BLENDER...
...AND I DROWNED 'IM...
...IN A BOILING POT OF CURRY.
NOPE, NOPE, NOPE.
—DIDN'T NEED THAT LAST PART.

CARROT

The Way of the Househusband

CHAPTER 78

PHEW!
MR. LANDLORD.
I SEE YOU'RE STRUGGLIN' WITH SOME BAD SEEDS WHO'VE TAKEN ROOT IN YOUR TURF.
OH, HELLO, MR. TATSU.
I'LL BACK YOU UP.
SHIBAINU
I'LL EVEN ROUND UP SOME EXTRA MUSCLE...

KNCH
YOU NEED SOME GUYS WEEDED OUT?
I GOTCHU, FAM!
YOU TAKE THAT SIDE!
THIS IS WAR!
WEEDS
SHIBAINU

GYAAAH!
WHAT'S WRONG ?!
BASTARDS! THEY WERE PACKIN'! THESE WEEDS... THEY'RE ALL THORNY!
WEEDS

BRING IT ON!
DUMB-ASS!
NEVER UNDER-ESTIMATE A THORNY WEED!
THIS AIN'T A BAREFISTED BRAWL.
WE GOTTA GEAR UP TOO!
HEH HEH... THAT'S YOUTHFUL SPIRIT FOR YA!

WEEDS
SHIBAINU

HFF!
HFF!
!
I DEALT WITH THE GUYS OVER HERE...
... BOSS!
DAMN IT, KID, YA DIDN'T PULL OUT THE ROOTS.
THESE GUYS SPROUT BACK IN NO TIME...
...UNLESS YA ROOT OUT EVERY LAST ONE.

MIX SOME VIN-EGAR...
I'LL FINISH 'EM OFF...
...AND DETER-GENT.
...WITH A SPRAY OF BULLETS FROM *THIS*!
SPECIAL HERBICIDE #1
WHOA. YOU CAN USE VINEGAR LIKE THAT?
THE ACIDITY OF VINEGAR MAKES IT AN EFFECTIVE WEED KILLER.
NOT ONLY IS IT EASY TO MAKE, IT'S SAFE TO USE AROUND KIDS AND PETS!

SPRITZ
SPRITZ
WSH

HOW D'YA LIKE *THEM* APPLES?!
NICE SHOOTIN', BOSS!
...
THIS STUFF...
...IS PRETTY STINKY.

HEY, BOYS...
LET'S TAKE FIVE, SHALL WE?
YOU SHOWED 'EM TODAY, BOSS!
SWEET!
I MADE US A VINEGAR DRINK.
VINEGAR AGAIN?
PEE-YEW!

OHO!
IS THIS APPLE CIDER VINEGAR?
THAT'S A FUN LITTLE COCK-TAIL.
THE CITRIC ACID IN VINEGAR BOTH BOOSTS ENERGY AND HELPS CONTROL BLOOD SUGAR.
THE ANTIOXIDANTS ARE GOOD FOR THE SKIN AND PREVENT OSTEOPOROSIS.
BUT IMBIBE WITH CAUTION. TOO MUCH OF THIS STUFF WILL MESS YOU UP...YOUR ESOPHAGUS AND STOMACH, TO BE EXACT.
IT'LL ERODE THE ENAMEL RIGHT OFF YOUR TEETH TOO, SO ORAL CARE IS INDIS-PENSABLE AFTER-WARD...

SHIBAINU
NOT A FAN.

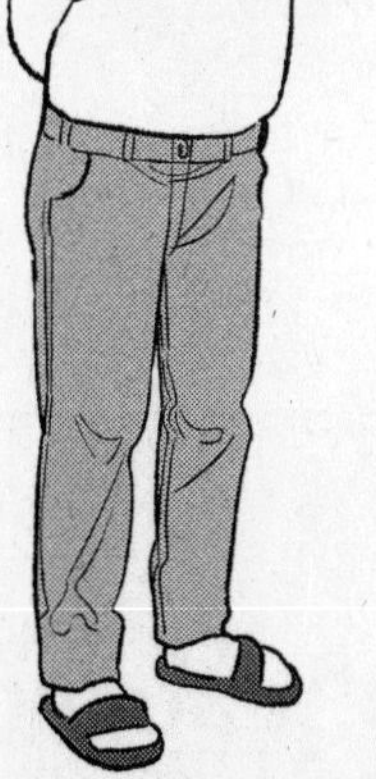

The Way of the Househusband

CHAPTER 79

MY RHINOCEROS BEETLE IS STRONGER!
NUH-UH. MY STAG BEETLE'S TOTALLY STRONGER!
NOW, NOW, BOYS. DON'T FIGHT.
WHAT *DO YOU* THINK, MR. TATSU?!
THE RHINO BEETLE IS THE HEAD HONCHO OF ALL THE BUGS.
DEFY HIM, AND YOU'LL NEVER MAKE THE CUT IN THE FOREST.

CREPES
HA!
THE HEAD HONCHO OF BUGS ?!
DON'T MAKE LIGHT OF STAG BEETLES!
EVER BEEN CAUGHT IN THEIR MAN-DIBLES?
NO LIE, THOSE THINGS WILL SEND YOUR PINKY FLYING!
NOW YER JUST EXAG-GERATIN'.

YOU TRYIN' TA PICK A FIGHT WITH THE CHAMPION OF INSECTS, PAL?
IF YOU DON'T EVEN KNOW WHAT STAG BEETLES ARE CAPABLE OF, YOU OUGHTA WALK AWAY NOW, *AMATEUR*.
WAM
A STAG BEETLE COULD NEVER BEAT A HEAVY-WEIGHT RHINO BEETLE, BASED ON SIZE ALONE!
IF WE'RE TALKIN' SIZE, YOU WANNA HAVE YOUR PINKY CUT OFF BY A STAG BEETLE'S GIANT MANDIBLES?!

FORGET IT, MR. TATSU. I DON'T CARE *THAT* MUCH.
OH NO. THERE'S NO BACKIN' DOWN AFTER ALL THE SHADE THIS PUNK THREW.
SHIBAINU
DON'T WORRY, SHORT STUFF—I'LL BRING YOU HIS HEAD!
NO THANKS.
LET THE BUG WARS BEGIN.
ARE THEY EVEN LISTEN-ING?

SO THIS IS THE FIGHTER? I LIKE THE CUT OF HIS JIB.
COOL, RIGHT?!
WELL, MR. RHINO ...
LET ME SHOW YA WHAT THE FAMILY'S BACKIN' CAN DO FOR YA.

WHAT'S *THAT*? YOU MADE SOME-THING?
I BOILED DOWN BROWN SUGAR AND *SHOCHU* TO MAKE SOME BEETLE FOOD.
THIS'LL HAVE HIM FLYIN' HIGH!
I HAVE BEETLE JELLY ALREADY THOUGH.
GET 'IM!
KICK SOME ASS!
TRAIN, TRAIN, AND TRAIN SOME MORE!

A TOAST TO OUR FUTURE CHAMP WITH SOME TOP-SHELF CREPES!
I GOTTA SAVE ROOM FOR DINNER.
THAT STAG BEETLE'S GONNA TAKE US TO THE TOP...
... AIN'T HE, SHORT STUFF?!
CAN YOU PLEASE LEAVE NOW?
MA'AM! ME AN' TAKUYA...
...ARE GONNA TURN THE FOREST'S POWER STRUCTURE UPSIDE DOWN!
OH, I SEE. THE FOREST'S ...
TAKUYA, WHO IS THIS PERSON?

DIDN'T THINK YOU'D SHOW AFTER PICKIN' A FIGHT WITH THE RHINO.
YOUR FIGHTER'S JUST SOME BUM. A RHINO IN NAME ONLY!

WASTE 'IM, DAGGER!
SLICE 'IM IN TWO, BLADE!
GEEZ, THESE GROWN-UPS HAVE A LOT OF ENERGY.
IT'S A MIYAMA STAG BEETLE.
READYYY ...
... FIGHT!

WHAM
NICE!
THAT'S THE WAY! PUNCH HIS LIGHTS OUT!
SEND 'IM BACK TO THE CLINK!
SO WEIRD.

GRP
AH! THE STAG BEETLE CLIMBED ON TOP.
NOW! GO!
MAGNUM UNDERARM THROW!
HA! GOT 'EM!
USE FINGER-CUTTING GUILLOTINE!

FLAP
FLAP
BZZ
BZZZZ

Run away!!

The Way of the Househusband

CHAPTER 80

UEKANAMONO CORPORATION
NING
METALWARE STORES LIKE MINE...
...ARE GETTING FEWER SHOPPERS THESE DAYS.
IT'S THE SAME AT MY WOMEN'S CLOTHING STORE.
WELL, YOU CAN BUY JUST ABOUT ANYTHING AT A SHOPPING MALL THESE DAYS...
IT'S A SIGN OF THE TIMES, I S'POSE.
THAT AIN'T RIGHT.
POPS, YOUR BLADES ARE THE BEST!

THEY'RE MUSCLIN' IN ON YER TURF. YA CAN'T TAKE THAT LYIN' DOWN!
M-MR. TATSU?! WHAT ARE YOU PLANNING TO DO?!
THOK
I MAY NOT LOOK IT...
...BUT I DID DABBLE IN DEALIN' BACK IN THE DAY. THAT'S RIGHT...I WAS A STREET HAWKER!

STEP ON UP! DON'T BE SHY !!!
UNLESS YER IN A HURRY...
...I SUGGEST YA STICK AROUND AN' HAVE A LISTEN!!!
HUH? WHAT? WHAT'S HE DOING?
ANAMONO CORPORATION

WHAT'S GOING ON?
A SALES DEMON-STRATION?
NOW, WHAT I'VE GOT HERE IS...
WA
...YER ALL-PURPOSE BLADE!
SOURCED IN JAPAN ...
...AT THE BOTTOM OF A MOUNTAIN WITH PURE SOIL AND WATER!
THIS AIN'T YER ORDINARY STEEL!

KLATR
DULL BLADES HAVE SHARP TIPS AND A HEEL THAT WON'T CUT.
BUT A REAL BLADE CAN CUT THROUGH BAMBOO!
IT WON'T BEND!
IT WON'T BREAK!
AND EVEN AFTER ALL THAT USE, THE TIP IS IN TIP-TOP SHAPE!
SCARY!

WHO WANTS...
...A NICE, SHARP BLADE?!
SHIBAINU
TOUGH SQUASH!
SHNK
SWF
SOFT TOMATOES!
APPLE PEELS!
THIS BABY SLICES ANYTHING LIKE A KNIFE THROUGH BUTTER!

SWIP
IT'S PERFECT FOR FILLETIN' FISH!
THNK
USE IT FOR ATONE-MENT!
USE IT FOR YER NEXT HIT!
LUNGE
YOU CAN EVEN USE IT FOR CHOPPIN' UP CHICKEN WITH THE SKIN STILL ON!
SLSH
STEP ON UP AND TRY IT FOR YOUR-SELVES!
THERE WAS SOME SKETCHY STUFF MIXED IN THERE.
UEKANAMONO CORPORATION
I'LL TAKE ONE!

WAP
COME GET 'EM CHEAP!
AS I ALWAYS SAY, STRIKE WHILE THE IRON IS HOT!
BUT A LITTLE TUSSLE CAN SPARK A GANG WAR...
...AND NEXT THING YA KNOW, THE COPS ARE COMIN' TO CATCH YOU!
TAKATSU
WOMEN'S FASHIO
INU
IF YOU DON'T WANNA GET COLLARED, START BY WEARIN' ONE A THESE!
POLICURE SWEATERS!
SIX THOUSAND YEN A POP!
CRIME-CATCH POLICURE!

WAP
WAP
WINTER'S A COMIN'!
HOW ABOUT A SWEATER TA GEAR UP YER FAMILY?!
BAINU
ALL RIGHT!
I'LL KNOCK IT DOWN TA FIVE THOU FOR YA!
PER-FECT FOR LOUN-GIN' AT HOME!
SHOPPING DOWN-TOWN!
AND ATTENDIN' LOW-KEY SHINDIGS!
THIS VERSATILE SWEATER TURNS YA INTO A SUPER-HERO...
...EVEN THE YAKUZA WOULD CLEAR THE WAY FOR!

THAT'S ...
...LAST SEASON'S MERCH, ISN'T IT?
!!!
WHAT'S THIS NOW?
WHO'S THAT?

HEY, I AIN'T SELLIN' FOR CHUMP CHANGE!
FINE, I'LL GIVE YA A DIS-COUNT!
FOUR THOU-SAND YEN!
OH SNAP!
FOUR!
CAN I GET A FOUR THOU-SAND?!
RIME♥CATCH POLICURE
SIGH ...
ARE YOU EVEN TRYING?

ALL RIGHT, YOU WIN!
I'LL MAKE IT BOGO! TAKE IT AND SCRAM, YA THIEF!!!
CRIME-CATCH POLICURE
WHOOSH
SOLD.
YEAH!

YOU'RE GONNA RUN ME OUTTA BUSINESS HAGGLIN' LIKE THAT, KID.
HEH!
FUN FACT...
THE VERSION OF THE *POLICURE* SWEATER THAT DEPICTS THE NEW MAGICAL GIRL ALONE IS ACTUALLY A PRETTY RARE FIND DUE TO ITS LIMITED PRODUCTION RUN.
AFTER IT PROVED MORE POPULAR THAN EXPECTED, ADDITIONAL SWEATERS WERE PRODUCED, BUT THEIR QUALITY DIDN'T MATCH UP TO THE ORIGINAL PRODUCT.
PLEASURE DOIN' BUSI-NESS!
CLASP

PHEW!
I GOT OUT OF WORK EARLY TODAY.
I-IS THAT A MIDNIGHT POLICE SWEATER?!
WHAT A LEGEND...

CRIME-CATCH POLICURE

The Way of the Househusband

THIS IS WHAT THE YOUNG FOLKS ARE INTO THESE DAYS?
GOTTA KEEP APPRISED OF THE LATEST TRENDS TO PROTECT YER HUSTLE, BOSS.
CHAPTER 81
HERE YOU ARE!
ONE LOVE BEAM OMELET RICE.

OKAY, MASTERS!
ARE YOU READY TO REPEAT THE MAGIC WORDS AFTER ME ?!
MAGICAL MEOW-MEOW POWER!
M-MAGICAL MEOW-MEOW...
... POWER!
NN... MEOW MEOW...
NN... MEOW MEOW?
LOVE MAKES FOOD TASTIER ON OUR PLATES!
SHIBAINU
LOVE BEAM, LOVE BEAM, ACTIVATE!

HIYA, EVERYONE!
WE HAVE A SPECIAL MAGICAL CAFE PERFORMANCE FOR YOU TODAY!
WE HOPE YOU'LL ENJOY IT!
OOOH! YEAH!
YEAH!
YEAH!
WHAT'S GOING ON?!
IS IT SOME NEW KIND A HIT?!

OOOH!
YEAH!!!
SHIBAINU
YEAH!
YEAH!!!

HFF... HFF...
WHAT WAS THAT PERFOR-MANCE ABOUT?
HFF... HFF...
THEY CALL THAT LIVE MUSIC, BOSS.
LIVE MUSIC?
I DON'T SEE HOW JINGI TEI CAN COMPETE WITH THAT.
IT'S NOT AS THOUGH I KNOW ANYONE I COULD ASK TO PERFORM.
IF IT'S CON-TACTS YOU NEED...
...I HAPPEN TO KNOW A GUY IN THE MUSIC BIZ...

JINGI TEI IS MY GO-TO LUNCH BREAK LOCATION.
JINGI TEI
HOUSE OF HONOR
CAFE
IT'S MY TIME TO RELAX.
THE RETRO ATMOSPHERE.
LUNCH SPECIALS THAT NEVER LEAVE ME DISAPPOINTED.
THE POST-MEAL COFFEE IS PLEASING TOO...
BMM CHA BMM BMM BMM CHA ♫
HMM?

CHECK ONE, TWO, YO!
HEY, HOW'S IT HANGIN'? G GODA IN DA HOUSE.
BAM
S'TIME TO DROP SOME BEATS. JINGI TEI, IT'S GOT GOOD EATS.
FO' TWENNY LONG YEARS, IT'S BEEN ON THIS STREET.
HEY, YO!
OKAY, THAT'S DIFFERENT.

WITH HONOR EVER UNCHANGIN', THIS GENT'S BEEN FIGHTIN' AN' SLAYIN'. A DOPE REP HE NOW GAININ'.
TWO DECADES IN THE BIZ, DAMN, THAT'S HELLA TENACIOUS.
ANY RECOMMEN-DATIONS YOU WANNA MAKE FO' US?
OMELET RICE.
FLUFFY EGGS TO BRING OUT THAT MAGIC. THE PRESENTA-TION'S ALWAYS DYNAMIC.
OVERALL, THAT DISH IS JUST CLASSIC.
THE MEALS, THEY COME WITH COFFEE. A CUP TA LEND SOME COLOR TO YOUR STORY.
THIS OWNER, HE'S GONNA TURN 20 INTO 40!
AAAIGHT!

MAKE SOME NOIIIISE!
CLAP CLAP
CLAP
GODA. GODA.
SMALL CHANGE OF PLANS.
COULD YOU SHOWCASE A NEW ADDITION TO THE MENU FOR ME TOO?
THE ADULT CREAMY PARFAIT.
YO, YO!
HUH? CREAM... PARFAIT?

HOMIE JUST DISHED UP A THEME. DUDE'S GOT THE BIGGEST BALLS I'VE EVER SEEN. MY HEART'S RACIN' AS I THINK UP MY NEXT RHYME SCHEME.
THE NEW CREAMY PARFAIT'S, UH...THE DESSERT OF YOUR DREAMS.
UH...IT'S A PARFAIT WITH FRUIT AND...
...WHIPPED CREAM?
OH, ACTUALLY, IT DOESN'T HAVE ANY FRUIT.
NO FRUIT... HUH? CAN YOU CALL THAT A PARFAIT?
UUUH... SO...ITS SWEETNESS WILL BLOW YOU AWAY.
FO' REAL... UH... BUY ONE TODAY.
ACTUALLY, IT ISN'T VERY SWEET EITHER.

WAM
YOU'RE MAKIN' THIS TOO HARD!
HOW WAS I SUPPOSED TO KNOW THAT?!
YOU KEEP INTER-RUPTING ...
...AND IT'S MAKIN' ME PANIC!
KOFF!
OH! *ER*... SORRY ABOUT THAT.

GREAT. WHATEVER THAT WAS SEEMS TO BE OVER.
NOW I CAN RELAX...
I'M TAKIN' OVER THE MIC TO LAY DOWN MORE RHYMES.
THE NAME'S TATSU AND I WORK HERE PART-TIME.
I'M A FULL-TIME HOUSE-HUSBAND.
INTO BATTLE I WEAR THIS HERE APRON.
DAMN IT. HERE WE GO AGAIN.
SHIBAINU

OUR NEWEST ADDITION IS THIS CREAMY ...
...ADULT PARFAIT.
IT'LL HAVE FAT STACKS OF CASH ROLLIN' INTO OUR CAFE.
THE SECRET'S THIS WHITE STUFF, THE CREAM.
ONE DOLLOP IS THE ACE UP OUR SLEEVE.
THESE PLANTS WILL HAVE YA FLYIN' HIGH.
THE MATCHA GREEN TEA. THAT'S WHAT I MEANT TO IMPLY.
IT'S SURE TA BE A HIT, SO GIVE IT A TRY.
WHAT? DON'T TELL ME THE OWNER'S GOING TO RAP TOO!

THE WAY OF THE HOUSEHUSBAND 9 END

MOROMI
ENZYME

The Way of the Househusband

MORNING ROUTINE OF A TWENTYSOMETHING JOB-HOPPER
WAKE UP
4:00 P.M.
A BIT OF A LATE RISER.
BRUSH TEETH
4:05 P.M.
HE CAN TAKE IT SLOW TODAY BECAUSE HE GOT FIRED YESTERDAY.

BREAKFAST
4:30 P.M.
HAD A GENIUS IDEA—SET UP BAMBOO SHOOTS FOR NAGASHI SOMEN.

BREAKFAST
5:00 P.M.
HAVING A LITTLE LIE-DOWN BECAUSE THE SETUP COLLAPSED PARTWAY THROUGH.

BREAKFAST
8:00 P.M.
SICK OF EVERYTHING.

EDITING VIDEOS
HIT... THAT... SUB... SCRIBE... BUTTON.

The Way of the Househusband

I SAW A BUNCH OF PEOPLE IN YUKATA ON MY WAY HOME FROM WORK TODAY.
OH, YEAH. THERE'S THAT FIREWORKS SHOW TONIGHT.
THE CROWDS AT THOSE ARE SO EXHAUST-ING.
I DON'T KNOW WHY SO MANY PEOPLE GO TO THEM.
SECURIN' A GOOD SPOT IS ALWAYS A BATTLE TOO.
BOOM
!!!

SOUNDS LIKE IT'S STARTIN'.
BOOM
BOOM
YUP.
BOOM
BOOM
BANG
FWOOOO
BOOM
BOOM
BOOM
BOOM
KRAKL
KRAKL
POP
SWUF

CAN'T SEE ANYTHING. I GUESS IT WAS A LONG SHOT.
MAYBE FROM THE ENTRANCE SIDE?
SHIBAINU
BOOM
BANG
DAMN. WE CAN ONLY GET A PEEK.
YEAH ...
BOOM
BOOOM
OUGHT TO GET A GOOD VIEW OF THE ACTION FROM THIS PARK...
BLAM
A LI'L MORE THIS WAY!

HFF! HFF!
HFF! HFF!
HFF! HFF!
HFF! HFF!
HUH?
IS IT OVER?
I DON'T HEAR ANY-THING.

BOOOM
!!!
IT'S COMIN' FROM THE SHOPPING DISTRICT!
HURRY!

WE KEPT RUNNING...
...RECK-LESSLY CHARG-ING AHEAD.
WE DIDN'T WANT TO SEE THE FIRE-WORKS BADLY ENOUGH TO GO TO THE ACTUAL SHOW...
...BUT WE AT LEAST WANTED TO SEE A LITTLE BIT.
THE MORE WE CHASED THEM...
WAIT!
THAT WAY!
...THE MORE WE WENT PAST THE POINT OF NO RETURN.
IT WAS THAT KIND OF SUMMER MEMORY.

FOR-
GET
IT.

The Way of the Househusband

Café NOIR
CRIME♡CATCH
POLICURE☆
Café NOIR
WOOSH
Tea Time

WOOSH
ZWSH
SWSH

WELL, THAT PUT A DAMPER...
...ON MY LUNCH BREAK.

The Way of the Househusband

BONUS MANGA ④ SEEKING FREEDOM

LIFE IS HARD. SEE YOU AGAIN IN VOLUME 10.

STAFF- MIDORINO, HIROE SPECIAL THANKS - YOSHIAKE SUKENO SENSEI, KIM

By the way, my pet Shiba
Inu's name is Daifuku,
after the Japanese sweet.
Because he's round like one.

KOUSUKE OONO

Kousuke Oono began his professional manga career in 2016 in the manga magazine *Monthly Comics @ Bunch* with the one-shot "Legend of Music." Oono's follow-up series, *The Way of the Househusband*, is the creator's first serialization as well as his first English-language release.

The Way of the House Husband

VOLUME 9

VIZ SIGNATURE EDITION

STORY AND ART BY
KOUSUKE OONO

TRANSLATION: Amanda Haley
ENGLISH ADAPTATION: Jennifer LeBlanc
TOUCH-UP ART & LETTERING: Bianca Pistillo
DESIGN: Alice Lewis
EDITOR: Jennifer LeBlanc

Printed in the U.S.A.

Published by VIZ Media, LLC
P.O. Box 77010
San Francisco, CA 94107

10 9 8 7 6 5 4 3 2 1
First printing, February 2023

1
S'time to drop some beats. Jingi Tei, it's got good eats.
Fo' twenny long years, it's been on this street (hey yo).

With honor ever unchangin', this gent's been fightin' an' slayin'.
A dope rep he now gainin'.

Two decades in the biz. Damn, that's hella tenacious.
Any recommendations you wanna make fo' us?

"Omelet rice." Fluffy eggs to bring out the magic.
The presentation's always dynamic. Overall, that dish is just classic.

The meals, they come with coffee. A cup ta lend some color to your story.
This owner, he's gonna turn 20 into 40!

2
My list of its charms ain't complete. Jingi Tei, it's got good eats.
Fo' twenny long years, it's been on this street.

A menu that don't need changin'. Self-service water refills exchangin'.
Even the reviews got no complainin'.

Two decades in the biz, that's hella tenacious.
Any dope lunch recs you wanna make fo' us?

"Omelet rice." Lunch comes with a seasonal salad on the side.
Plus soup that'll have your eyes goin' wide.
If it's eggs ya want, he's happy to provide. (Damn straight!)

The meals, they come with coffee. A cup ta lend some color to your story.
This owner, he's gonna turn 20 into 40!

3
Runnin' out of things t' say, I'm on repeat. Jingi Tei, it's got good eats.
Fo' twenny long years it's been on this street.

This cafe's gonna go on unchangin'. Always stayin' cool and entertainin'.
Into the future, it'll be remainin'.

Two decades in the biz, that's hella tenacious.
Anythin' else you wanna say to us?

"Ahem, well then, I have to shout out a new addition to the menu.
It's called the Adult Creamy Parfait. It's a bitter parfait, and the
secret ingredient is matcha. Make it a combo with cake for a discount.
I hope you'll check it out. Also, completely unrelated, the shopping
district is holding its annual stamp rally again this year. If you have
a meal here, we'll stamp your sheet, so if you're interested in that,
please check it out as well."

Whoa, whoa, that's way too long. You gotta keep it short.

The meals, they come with coffee.
A cup ta lend some color to your story.
This owner, he's gonna turn 20 into 40!

Jingi Tei, it's got good eats.
Fo' twenny long years it's been on this street.

Lyrics: G Goda

HEY
YO

Six short stories that set the scene for the best-selling *BEASTARS* series!

BEAST COMPLEX

Story and Art by **Paru Itagaki**

In these six stories from the creator of the Eisner-nominated, best-selling series BEASTARS, a menagerie of carnivores and herbivores grapple with conflicts based on their differences and—sometimes—find common ground.

RATED T+ OLDER TEEN

VIZ